SCIENTIFIC RIVALRIES
AND SCANDALS

THE RACE
TO DISCOVER
THE AIDS
VIRUS

LUC MONTAGNIER
VS ROBERT GALLO

STUART A. KALLEN

Twenty-First Century Books
Minneapolis

Twenty-First Century Books
A division of Lerner Publishing Group, Inc.
241 First Avenue North
Minneapolis, MN 55401 U.S.A.

Website address: www.lernerbooks.com

Library of Congress Cataloging-in-Publication Data

Kallen, Stuart A., 1955–
    The race to discover the AIDS virus : Luc Montagnier vs Robert Gallo / By Stuart A. Kallen.
        p.   cm.— (Scientific rivalries and scandals)
    Includes bibliographical references and index.
    ISBN 978–0–7613–5490–1 (lib. bdg. : alk. paper)
    1. AIDS (Disease)—Juvenile literature. 2. HIV (Viruses)—History—Juvenile literature. 3. Gallo, Robert C.—Juvenile literature. 4. Montagnier, Luc.—Juvenile literature. I. Title.
QR201.A37K35 2013
614.5'99392—dc23

                                                        22010039375

Manufactured in the United States of America
1 – MG – 7/15/12

CONTENTS

MYSTERY

DISEASE

Television cameras rolled and reporters from around the world waited anxiously at a press conference in Washington, D.C., on April 23, 1984.

Surrounded by the nation's leading research scientists, Margaret Heckler, U.S. Health and Human Services (HHS) secretary, walked to the podium to announce magnificent news. "The probable cause of AIDS [acquired immunodeficiency syndrome] has been found," she said.

By this point, the terrifying and deadly disease known as AIDS had spread to at least five continents and had killed more than four thousand people. People with AIDS suffered from devastating infections and rare cancers and often died agonizing deaths. In the United States, AIDS mostly targeted gay (homosexual) men and drug users.

Heckler told the crowd that after years of research, scientists had found that AIDS was caused by a virus called HTLV-3. In sharing the news of this discovery, Heckler also informed her listeners that for the very first time, doctors had a blood test for detecting AIDS that would soon become available.

As she wrapped up her historic press conference, Heckler added, "In particular, credit must go to our eminent Dr. Robert Gallo, chief of the National Cancer Institute Laboratory of Tumor Cell Biology, who directed the research that produced this discovery."

As Americans rejoiced at the news, some of the most prominent doctors and researchers in France watched Heckler's press conference in stunned disbelief. About eleven months earlier, French virologist (a scientist who studies viruses) Luc Montagnier of the Pasteur Institute in Paris, France, had published an article in a respected scientific journal. In it, he stated that he had discovered the virus that caused AIDS. The Pasteur Institute charged that

At the 1984 press conference announcing the discovery of the AIDS virus, both HHS secretary Margaret Heckler *(left)* and U.S. scientist Robert Gallo *(right)* spoke to reporters.

French virologist Luc Montagnier works in his research lab at the Pasteur Institute in Paris, France, in the mid-1980s.

Robert Gallo had falsely taken credit for Montagnier's discovery. This charge launched a long-running and fierce rivalry for credit for a major scientific breakthrough.

A COMPLEX, COMPELLING STORY

Heckler's announcement of an AIDS blood test was indeed cause for celebration. Not only had almost two thousand Americans died of AIDS by 1984, but one hundred new U.S. cases were being reported every week. For the first time since 1981, when AIDS had surfaced as a frightening public health hazard, people with the illness and those who cared for them had hope. They knew that the more scientists could learn about the virus that caused AIDS, the better the chances for development of a treatment and, most importantly, a cure for the disease.

The battle over who would be credited for discovering the AIDS virus is a complex and compelling story. It involves exciting and sophisticated microbiology, huge scientific egos, the coveted Nobel Prize in Medicine, and great amounts of money. The dispute also involved tense congressional investigations and delicate negotiations between the presidents of the United

States and France. As a scientific controversy filled with mystery, deception, conspiracies, and hope, the race to discover the AIDS virus is a riveting, human tale.

STRANGE SYMPTOMS

In the fall of 1979, a thirty-six-year-old New York City schoolteacher named Rick Wellikoff was frightened by unusual purple blotches on his skin. The blotches were painless, but they refused to heal. Wellikoff also had swollen lymph nodes. These small, bean-shaped internal organs, distributed throughout the body, are central to the human immune system—the system that fights disease. Among many functions, lymph nodes kill blood cells that make tumors. They also prevent pathogens (disease-producing bacteria and viruses) from multiplying in the body.

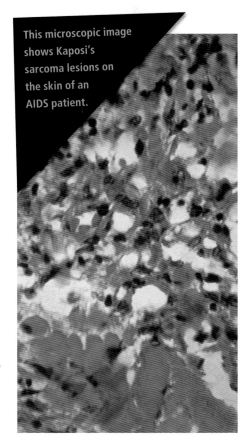

This microscopic image shows Kaposi's sarcoma lesions on the skin of an AIDS patient.

In September Wellikoff visited Dr. Linda Laubenstein. She found that he had a rare skin cancer called Kaposi's sarcoma, or KS. The condition was very unusual. Few doctors had studied or written about it. When Laubenstein tried to learn more about KS, she discovered that it was first described in 1871. It normally affected elderly men of European Jewish or Mediterranean descent. In 108 years, doctors had recorded only about 650 cases of KS worldwide.

Laubenstein wondered how a relatively young American man had contracted such a rare cancer.

The previously healthy schoolteacher had nothing that stood out in his background—except for one thing. He was gay. Laubenstein contacted other doctors in the region. She found that another man, an unnamed thirty-seven-year-old model, also had KS. The model knew Wellikoff, and they had a mutual friend, Gaëtan Dugas. Dugas also had the unusual blotches on his skin. Dugas was a gay Canadian flight attendant who traveled the world for his job. In later interviews, he said that he was extremely sexually active. He boasted of having hundreds of sexual partners a year.

Compared to other cancers, KS is relatively mild. It typically grows very slowly and takes many years to kill its victims. However, Wellikoff's KS was very aggressive, and he died on December 23, 1980. Doctors were baffled. The odds of a North American contracting KS were about 1 in 1.5 million. The odds that three acquaintances would be afflicted with the same type of rare cancer were even greater. Although no one knew it at the time, Wellikoff, the unnamed model, and Dugas were among the first North Americans to die of AIDS.

Dr. Michael Gottlieb, shown here with a model of a cell infected with human immunodeficiency virus (HIV), first discovered that AIDS was destroying patients' T cells.

TELLTALE T CELLS

In November 1980, about a month before Rick Wellikoff's death, another medical mystery appeared in Los Angeles, California. Michael Gottlieb, an immunologist, a doctor who studies the immune system, was conducting research at the University of California–Los Angeles (UCLA). Gottlieb learned of a thirty-one-year-old male artist who had a severe yeast infection in his throat. The infection, called florid candidiasis, makes breathing extremely difficult. The case was very strange, since only babies born with defective immune systems were known to suffer with this condition.

Gottlieb obtained a small sample of the patient's lung tissue and had it analyzed. Testing revealed that the patient had a very low number of T cells. First discovered in the late 1970s, T cells are white blood cells that play a key role in the body's immune system. Some T cells trigger other blood cells to create antibodies, which are proteins that destroy disease-causing pathogens. Other T cells tell the immune system when the threat from a pathogen has passed.

The case of the patient with low T cells was extraordinary. None of Gottlieb's colleagues had ever heard of a disease that specifically killed white blood cells. Gottlieb studied the man's health charts and learned that he had repeatedly contracted sexually transmitted diseases such as gonorrhea and syphilis. The man also mentioned that he was gay, but the doctor did not think this had anything to do with the patient's illness.

About six months later, an extremely sick advertising agent made an appointment with Dr. Joel Weisman in Los Angeles. Weisman, who himself

Dr. Joel Weisman saw gay male patients with swollen lymph nodes and other alarming symptoms in the early 1980s.

was gay, had many gay patients. The advertising agent had a number of frightening symptoms unlike any Dr. Weisman had ever seen. The patient's fingernails were surrounded by a white fungus; a yeast infection was growing out of control in his throat; and he suffered from drastic weight loss, skin rashes, and fevers. In addition, the advertising agent had abnormally swollen lymph nodes. About twenty other gay male patients Weisman had seen that year also had swollen lymph nodes.

Weisman diagnosed the ad agent with a rare illness called Pneumocystis carinii pneumonia (PCP). Previously, this affliction of the lungs was seen only in people with extremely weak immune systems, such as babies suffering from malnutrition.

Weisman referred the patient to Michael Gottlieb. At UCLA researchers discovered that the man was suffering from a loss of T cells. By May 1981, Gottlieb and Weisman had learned of several other PCP cases among gay men. They reported the information to the Centers for Disease Control and Prevention (CDC), headquartered in Atlanta, Georgia. This organization, part of the U.S. Department of Health and Human Services, works to protect public health in the United States. It gathers statistics, funds research, tracks epidemics (sudden outbreaks of a disease within a region or a large group of people), educates doctors and the public, and does other work to prevent and control the spread of disease in the United States.

FROM GRID TO AIDS

The CDC assigned Harold Jaffe to investigate the increase in PCP and KS in gay men. Jaffe was an epidemiologist, a scientist who studies the origins and spread of diseases. He was soon able to compile a list of young gay men who had contracted PCP. With this information, the CDC published the first official report on what would become the AIDS epidemic.

On June 5, 1981, the CDC newsletter stated that between October 1980 and May 1981, five young gay men in Los Angeles had been diagnosed with PCP. Two had already died. All of them also had a condition called cytomegalovirus (CMV), one of many herpes viruses.

At first U.S. president Ronald Reagan *(left)* was slow to react to the AIDS crisis. He eventually established a presidential commission on AIDS and made his first public speech about the disease in 1987.

The discovery of PCP and CMV in gay men was more than a public health crisis. It also set the stage for a thorny political issue. At the time, Ronald Reagan was president of the United States. He had the backing of powerful conservative Christian groups, many of which promoted an antigay agenda. The Reagan administration had little interest in funding research on an affliction affecting what appeared to be a small number of gay men.

Evidence of a major new health crisis continued to grow. By June 1982, the CDC had recorded three hundred cases of the puzzling new syndrome among gay men, most of them in New York City, Los Angeles, and San Francisco. The men appeared to be infecting one another through sexual contact.

Six months later, that number of cases had risen to six hundred, and 60 percent of the patients had died. Doctors noted that people with the syndrome experienced a host of deadly infections due to weakened immune systems. Most of the patients were gay or bisexual

"It's the worst way I've ever seen anybody go. I've seen young people die of cancer. But this is total body rot. It's merciless."

New York doctor treating early AIDS patients, 1982

PEOPLE WITH AIDS ALLIANCE

men (men who have sexual relations with both men and women). So at first, scientists called the syndrome gay-related immune deficiency, or GRID.

But while studying the outbreak, the CDC realized that not all GRID patients were gay or bisexual men. About 13 percent of patients were intravenous (IV) drug users, who used syringes to inject heroin and other drugs into their veins. The drug users seemed to be passing the disease to one another by sharing syringes containing infected blood. Another 6 percent of patients came from Haiti, an island nation in the Caribbean Sea. Of the Haitians, many were infants and children, indicating that the disease could be passed from mothers to babies. Less than 1 percent of people with the immune deficiency syndrome had hemophilia, a bleeding disorder. (The blood of people with hemophilia does not clot properly. In some cases, even minor cuts cause prolonged bleeding. In severe cases, hemophiliacs require regular blood transfusions to survive.) It appeared that the affected hemophiliacs were getting infected blood from blood banks where they received transfusions.

Because 25 percent of those suffering from GRID were heterosexuals (people who have sexual relations with those of the opposite sex), the CDC coined a new name to describe the group of related illnesses. In August 1982, GRID was renamed acquired immunodeficiency syndrome. AIDS encompassed a group of normally rare or minor illnesses that could be deadly for people with extremely weakened immune systems.

A MERCILESS KILLER

Once AIDS took hold, it weakened and wasted its victims quickly. As one unnamed patient explained, "I found myself bedridden with a cold that wouldn't go away, viral bronchitis, fever, diarrhea, loss of appetite, and extreme fatigue. Then I developed chronic ear infections, shingles [large, painful blisters] on the backs of both legs, and a persistent sore throat." Even the most hardened, experienced doctors were shaken by the suffering experienced by AIDS patients during their agonizing deaths. A New York physician stated, "It's the worst way I've ever seen anybody go. I've seen young people die of cancer. But this is total body rot. It's merciless."

As the epidemic spread, public health officials grew increasingly alarmed. "[AIDS] isn't going away," the CDC's Jim Curran told a meeting of gay health professionals in March 1982. "Even if we find a [cause], it will be considerable time, probably years, before we can develop a vaccine [preventive treatment] or some strategy to eradicate [get rid of] it. We are in for a long haul."

Doctors observed that the infection was spreading through sex, IV drug use, tainted blood supplies, and the birthing process. They suspected that whatever was making people sick was passing from one person to another through blood or other body fluids. But people who had contact with infected blood or body fluids didn't always get sick right away. It could take up to five years for a person to develop AIDS after infection. Whatever was causing AIDS was slow moving and was carried by blood. Doctors suspected a virus.

"[AIDS] isn't going away....It will be considerable time, probably years, before we can develop a vaccine or some strategy to eradicate [get rid of] it. We are in for a long haul."

Jim Curran, Centers for Disease Control and Prevention, 1982

CHAPTER TWO

THE VIRUS
HUNTERS

The word *virus* is Latin for "toxin" or "poison." The name fits because many viruses cause disease. Viruses are parasites—organisms that feed and live off other organisms.

Viruses cannot reproduce themselves. They can multiply only by invading healthy cells in other organisms, called hosts, and forcing the hosts to produce more of the virus.

All living cells, including the cells of viruses, contain deoxyribonucleic acid, or DNA. Each DNA molecule takes the shape of a long double helix, or double spiral. DNA contains genes, substances that determine which characteristics parents pass on to their children. People often compare DNA to a set of blueprints, a recipe, or a code because it holds the instructions for determining physical characteristics, such as gender, hair color, and eye color.

DNA also contains a recipe for building other components of cells, including ribonucleic acid, or RNA. RNA molecules are similar to DNA molecules, but they take the form of a single spiral instead of a double spiral. The function of RNA is to translate and carry out the genetic instructions stored in DNA.

Medical researchers joke that a virus is "a piece of nucleic acid [genetic material] surrounded by bad news." The bad news is the way in which viruses cause illness inside host organisms. A virus first attaches to healthy host cells. The genetic information in the virus's DNA then tricks the host cells into producing more virus molecules. The new virus molecules break free of the host cells, killing them. Then virions, or virus particles, invade other healthy cells, killing them too.

Because one virus molecule can reproduce thousands of new virions, viral infections can spread quickly throughout the body. With a human flu virus, for example, virions quickly attack cells in the nasal passages, throat, lungs, and muscles. This attack causes a runny nose, sore throat, cough, and body aches.

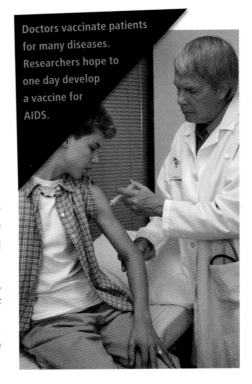

Doctors vaccinate patients for many diseases. Researchers hope to one day develop a vaccine for AIDS.

Viruses such as influenza, polio, mumps, and measles killed millions of people before the 1950s. But the development of vaccines considerably slowed the death rate from viruses. Vaccines are treatments that stimulate the immune system to fight and destroy viruses and bacteria. Scientists usually make vaccines from dead or very weak strains of the microbe they are trying to fight. For instance, flu vaccines are made from a weakened form of a flu virus. When someone gets a flu vaccine (through a shot or a mist spray), the weakened flu virus produces only mild flu symptoms or no symptoms in the person's body. At the same time, the vaccine triggers the person's immune system to produce antibodies to fight the weakened or dead virus. After this first attack, the immune system knows how to produce antibodies to fight and kill the same virus. The person has developed immunity against (resistance to) the virus. If it attacks again, it will not make the person sick.

CANCER AND VIRUSES

By the 1960s, a growing number of people around the world were dying of cancer. Cancer can attack the breasts, lungs, liver, colon, brain, blood, and other parts of the body. The disease causes cells to multiply out of control and invade healthy tissue. After enough tissue becomes cancerous, an organ or other part of the body stops working properly, often causing death.

In the early 1960s, some researchers suggested that slow-acting viruses might be the cause of cancers. While this was only a theory, the U.S. National Cancer Institute (NCI), part of the U.S. National Institutes of Health in Bethesda, Maryland, set up the Virus Cancer Program in 1964. By 1968 the U.S. government was giving the program major funding.

U.S. president Richard Nixon signs legislation in 1971 funding research on cancer. Finding the link between viruses and cancer would later help researchers identify the AIDS virus.

A VIRUS IN REVERSE

The most exciting development in virus-cancer research was led by Harry Rubin, a veterinarian. In the 1950s and the 1960s, he studied Rous sarcoma virus (RSV), which infects chickens. When Rubin infected a healthy chicken cell with RSV, it immediately turned into a cancer cell. This study showed a crucial link between viruses and cancer.

RSV creates cancer because it behaves differently than most viruses. When an ordinary virus reproduces, its DNA copies its genes to create RNA. The newly created RNA carries out genetic instructions stored in the DNA. But RSV works in reverse. Instead of its DNA copying its genes to create RNA, the virus's RNA creates its DNA. RSV contains a gene that causes sarcoma, a kind of cancer. When RSV copies the sarcoma gene to the DNA of a healthy cell, the cell becomes cancerous.

For the Rous virus to create DNA from RNA, it needs a special enzyme, a substance that brings about chemical reactions. In 1970 two virologists, Howard Termin and David Baltimore, isolated this enzyme in the Rous virus. They named it reverse transcriptase (RT) because it transcribes (writes down) genetic information in reverse, from RNA to DNA. They also called the Rous virus a retrovirus. (*Retro* means "backward" in Latin.)

With the discovery of RT in chickens, scientists could search human cells for the RT enzyme, which indicates the presence of a cancer-causing retrovirus. While not all retroviruses cause cancer, the link between the Rous virus and cancer placed RT research at the forefront of science.

GROWING CELL LINES

In 1971 Robert Charles Gallo was a junior researcher at the National Cancer Institute. He was working to find a retrovirus in humans. To do his work, Gallo needed to look at virions—some of the smallest visible particles on Earth. (It would take one quintillion, or one billion times one billion, virions to fill a Ping-Pong ball.) To observe the size, shape, and behavior of such tiny particles, Gallo and other virus hunters used electron microscopes. These microscopes use beams of electrons (atomic particles) rather than rays of light to illuminate objects too small to be seen with traditional microscopes. An electron microscope can magnify viruses more than fifty thousand times.

But the researchers also needed to study viruses in action. They accomplished this with a system called in vitro, a Latin term for "within the glass." An in vitro experiment is performed on cells, blood, or tissue that has been taken from an animal or human and put into glass test tubes, flasks, or petri dishes, where it continues to live. The living material is called a culture.

In vitro systems allow virologists to measure the amount of virus in a cell culture and to determine the type of healthy cells targeted by the virus. In vitro systems also allow scientists to watch while a virus kills a healthy cell or grossly alters its form and function.

Most in vitro cell cultures live for only a few days. These are called short-term cultures. However, for reasons not completely understood by scientists, some cell cultures grow and multiply indefinitely. These are called immortalized cell cultures. The resulting growth is called a cell line. Robert Gallo explained the importance of cell lines:

> It didn't take long for virologists (and other scientists) to realize the potential of the cell line as a research tool. If a virus could be transmitted to a cell line . . . the culture itself would consist of a single cell type continuously multiplying. The virus could be produced in a relatively pure form. And most important, the scientist would be assured of large enough quantities of virus, obtainable repeatedly, virtually on demand, to study the reproductive cycle of the virus and its chemical makeup.

FIGHTING
FOR HIS SISTER

Robert Gallo was known among his colleagues as a highly motivated virus hunter who spent long hours in the lab. His determination to cure disease came from his sister, Judy. When Gallo was eleven years old, five-year-old Judy died of childhood leukemia. Gallo was heartbroken. But he was also impressed by the hospitals and physicians who used the latest scientific methods to treat his sister. He later wrote, "Increasingly, I saw science as another kind of religion, certainly one that would yield more predictable results if one served it faithfully.

Robert Gallo rose to the top levels of U.S. medical organizations during his career.

Though I had seen firsthand the limitations of medicine, I had also seen another world, academic centers peopled by physicians who devoted their lives to trying to cure disease by perfecting their understanding of its mechanisms." In the years that followed, Gallo developed an intense interest in biology, medicine, and cancer. It was this determination and focus that led to Gallo's dramatic research on AIDS.

HUMAN T CELL LEUKEMIA

Gallo began by focusing on two animal retroviruses: one that caused leukemia in mice and another that caused leukemia in cats. Leukemia is a cancer of the blood that causes an abnormal increase in white blood cells. Gallo then began to look at cancerous T cells from people with leukemia. These cells multiply rapidly in the body of people with leukemia. But they refuse to grow in vitro, making them difficult to study. However, in 1975 researchers in Gallo's lab found a way to nurture cancerous T cells in vitro by feeding them a bean plant extract called phytohemagglutinin, or PHA. In 1976 Gallo announced this discovery in *Science*, the journal of the American Association for the Advancement of Science. Gallo called the bean plant substance T cell growth factor.

Gallo obtained a lymph node from Charles Robinson, who had died from a type of T cell skin cancer. Using tissue from the lymph node and T cell growth factor, technicians were able to grow cell lines of immortalized cancerous T cells in a flask. This process produced an endless quantity of cancerous T cells for study. Gallo's colleague Bernard Poiesz later tested Robinson's T cells for the enzyme RT, which would indicate the presence of a retrovirus. The cells tested positive for RT but in quantities that were too low to be considered scientifically important.

Nonetheless, Poiesz felt he had made an important discovery. He searched scientific publications to advance his research. He found a

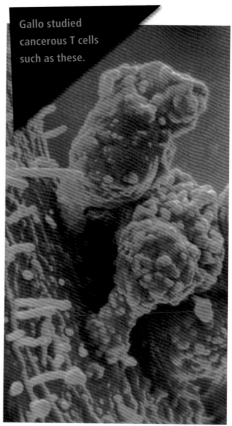

Gallo studied cancerous T cells such as these.

Japanese report that discussed a previously unknown disease called adult T-cell leukemia, or ATL. T cells from patients with this disease grew well in vitro, in a manner identical to Robinson's T cells, and they contained RT in larger quantities. This was evidence that a virus used RT to cause a rare type of leukemia. Excited by the data, Poiesz showed the results to Gallo, who suggested changing the name of ATL to the human T-cell leukemia virus, or HTLV. In the autumn of 1981, Gallo reported to the head of the NCI, Vince Devita, that his group had found clear-cut evidence that a retrovirus caused a rare form of human cancer.

While Gallo was struggling to link HTLV to cancer, the AIDS epidemic had just begun. When Gallo learned of AIDS, a slow-acting disease transmitted through infected blood, he suspected that it might be caused by HTLV. He intently studied the relationship of HTLV to AIDS throughout 1982.

> "Increasingly, I saw science as another kind of religion, certainly one that would yield more predictable results if one served it faithfully."
>
> Robert Gallo, 1991

CHAPTER THREE

THE FRENCH
CONNECTION

In the late 1970s and the early 1980s, doctors in western Europe also began to see patients with baffling, aggressive new diseases.

In Copenhagen, Denmark, a gay agricultural engineer in his thirties was stricken with PCP. In Cologne, Germany, doctors were puzzled by the case of a renowned young violinist, who traveled widely on the concert circuit. His lymph nodes expanded at a frightening rate before he contracted KS.

In France some doctors saw hopelessly sick patients who had connections to Africa. A heterosexual Portuguese cab driver in Paris, a man known only as M. Fel (to protect privacy, the French doctors did not use patients' full names), suffered from an incredible array of afflictions. Previously, he had served with the Portuguese military in the African nations of Angola, Mozambique, and Zaire (later called the Democratic Republic of the Congo). In Africa he had had sexual relationships with many local women. M. Fel's case came to the attention of thirty-four-year-old doctor Willy Rozenbaum at the Claude-Bernard Hospital in Paris. Rozenbaum observed that the patient had PCP. His mouth and throat were covered with a thick, white fungus. Enormous warts covered his entire body, including his arms and legs.

French doctor Willy Rozenbaum treated a patient with PCP and other AIDS-related symptoms in Paris, France, in the early 1980s.

Rozenbaum could not under-stand what was causing M. Fel's condition. Searching for answers, he called in his colleague Jacques Leibowitch, an immunologist. But before the doctors could take tests, M. Fel's brain became inflamed with an extremely rare infection and he died. Leibowitch wrote that the man had died from "a serious infection, still unknown, of African origin."

Soon after M. Fel's death, two women died of PCP in Paris hospitals. One of the women was from Zaire. The other was a Frenchwoman who had lived in central Africa and was married to a Zairian.

VIRUS HOTLINE

Rozenbaum was intensely concerned about the puzzling cases being reported in Europe. He was therefore very interested in a CDC newsletter that arrived in his office in June 1981. It contained an article about five young gay men treated for PCP in Los Angeles. The article led Rozenbaum to conclude that the cases of PCP were caused by a new type of virus.

On the same morning Rozenbaum received the CDC newsletter, he treated a man known only as V.M. A flight attendant for Air France, V.M.

traveled a great deal between Africa, Europe, and the Americas. He was very sexually active, with up to fifty male sex partners a year. V.M. exhibited a dry cough, a prolonged fever, weight loss, and enlarged lymph nodes.

Rozenbaum began an investigation to compile data about diseases contracted by gay men in France. He set up a telephone hotline for doctors to share information with him and distributed the number to medical facilities around Paris. Rozenbaum also hired an epidemiologist to join the study.

> "My [AIDS] patients are dying. I need a treatment."
>
> Dr. Willy Rozenbaum, 1982

TASK FORCE

In December 1981, Jacques Leibowitch read about several cases of KS in gay men in Los Angeles. Leibowitch called his sister, a professor of dermatology (the branch of medicine dealing with skin diseases) at a Paris hospital. She reported treating several gay men for KS. Like Rozenbaum, Leibowitch was convinced the illnesses afflicting gay men were caused by a virus.

Early in 1982, Leibowitch, Rozenbaum, and eight other doctors set up an informal task force to track the new disease. Between March 31 and December 31, 1982, the French task force counted twenty-nine patients, some with African connections, whose symptoms fit the profile of AIDS, as the CDC was by then calling the disease. At the same time, doctors across Europe were reporting an epidemic of patients with suppressed, or weakened, immune systems. The situation appeared to be growing dire. "My patients are dying," Rozenbaum implored his fellow doctors. "I need a treatment."[10]

Rozenbaum left the Claude-Bernard Hospital and took a new post at Pitié-Salpêtrière Hospital, also in Paris. He continued his work with the task force, meeting with the group about once a month. During the course of their discussions, Leibowitch mentioned Robert Gallo's study of retroviruses and the discovery of HTLV.

Soon after, Rozenbaum was invited to present a lecture at the Pasteur Institute. After the lecture, virologist Françoise Brun-Vezinet suggested that

Rozenbaum contact Jean-Claude Chermann and Luc Montagnier, who worked at the Pasteur Institute's Department of Virology. The focus of their work was to find a retrovirus that caused breast cancer. The Pasteur Institute had the technologies needed to conduct research on retroviruses, as well as supplies of retroviruses from cats and mice. Montagnier and Chermann agreed to let Rozenbaum use the Pasteur Institute's retrovirus laboratories for AIDS research.

Rozenbaum, Brun-Vezinet, Montagnier, Chermann, and Chermann's assistant Françoise Barré-Sinoussi began working together in early 1983. The researchers observed that a sharp decline in T cells in a patient indicated the first signs of AIDS, suggesting that AIDS was caused by a retrovirus that invaded and destroyed T cells. However, it seemed impossible to study infected T cells because the virus destroyed the cells.

Rozenbaum concluded that he needed to harvest T cells from an infected person before they were destroyed. With these cells, he could grow more infected T cells for study. He needed T cells from someone in the early stages

Left to right: Luc Montagnier, Jean-Claude Chermann, and Françoise Barré-Sinoussi were part of a French team working on AIDS research in 1983.

of AIDS, a condition called AIDS-related complex (ARC). People with ARC have symptoms associated with a weakened immune system, such as lymph node enlargement, fever, weight loss, and diarrhea, but their T cells have not yet been destroyed.

When fashion designer Frédéric Brugière visited Rozenbaum with enlarged lymph nodes, the doctor realized Brugière had ARC. He could provide the infected T cells that Rozenbaum needed.

REPRODUCING A RETROVIRUS

Rozenbaum surgically removed a small piece of tissue from one of Brugière's lymph nodes. He gave the tissue to Montagnier, who began working in his lab on the night of January 6, 1983. The virologist cut the tissue into small slices and placed them in a solution that separated the T cells from the other blood cells in the sample. He exposed some of the T cells to a protein extract taken from *Staphylococcus,* a bacterium that causes infection. The infection made the T cells grow.

Montagnier placed the T cells and their growth agent in an incubator, or heating chamber. He set the heat to 98.6°F (37°C), the temperature of the human body, which is ideal for growing cell cultures. According to Montagnier, "Then began a long wait. Every day, I would look at the culture under a microscope. [The cells] were multiplying well. Every three days . . . Françoise Barré-Sinoussi [would] look for the presence of a retrovirus."

Barré-Sinoussi was a meticulous technician who had previously worked with Robert Gallo. Her measurements of the growing cell culture showed that a retrovirus was reproducing rapidly in Brugière's T cells. She understood that something very important was happening in the flask.

The team then sent a small sample of Brugière's T cells to researcher Charles Dauguet, also at the Pasteur Institute. Montagnier described Dauguet's work: "With great patience, working hard for

"We were sure it was a retrovirus. For us there was no doubt."

Françoise Barré-Sinoussi, a virologist, remembering early work on identifying HIV, 2000 days on end, eyes glued to the [electron] microscope, he hunted for a cell—perhaps one in a hundred or one in a thousand—that might harbor the [retro] virus." Dauguet finally saw something that appeared to be the retrovirus they were looking for. He photographed it under the microscope. Although the photo was of poor quality, according to Barré-Sinoussi, "We were sure it was a retrovirus. For us there was no doubt."

At the same time, Montagnier and his team were in close contact with Robert Gallo and other AIDS researchers in the United States. Aware of Gallo's research, Montagnier obtained HTLV specimens from Gallo's lab. Montagnier wanted to photograph both the French retrovirus and the HTLV samples under an electron microscope to chart and compare their genetic makeup. But while Gallo was open about and willing to share information from his research, Montagnier kept news of the French retrovirus confidential at first.

THE BRU ROOM

In February 1983, Montagnier informed Rozenbaum of his lab's discovery. Because the viral agent had been found in Brugière's lymph nodes, Montagnier referred to the new virus as BRU—the first three letters of the patient's name. However, finding a virus in a single patient did not prove that BRU caused AIDS. The virologists at the Pasteur Institute needed to isolate BRU, along with the RT enzyme, in at least a dozen ARC patients to scientifically establish the link.

To continue their research, the virologists set up a lab called the BRU Room to study the virus. Rozenbaum sent tissue samples from additional ARC patients to the virologists, but the results of their studies were confusing. The studies showed that some patients were infected with both BRU and with Gallo's virus, HTLV. Even so, the French researchers were sure that HTLV was *not* the source of AIDS. HTLV caused T cells to multiply rapidly, creating leukemia. The BRU virus, on the other hand, killed T cells—and a decline in T cells was the first sign that a patient had AIDS. The French researchers were sure that BRU, not HTLV, was the cause of AIDS.

CHAPTER FOUR

GALLO VERSUS MONTAGNIER

In the United States, Robert Gallo and his colleagues at the National Cancer Institute were trying to link HTLV to AIDS.

In Paris, Luc Montagnier and his colleagues at the Pasteur Institute believed that BRU was the cause of AIDS. In February 1983, Montagnier decided to tell Robert Gallo about the French discovery of BRU. He sent Jacques Leibowitch to the United States with a letter informing Gallo of the discovery.

But unknown to Montagnier, Leibowitch also brought Gallo a thermos full of the Pasteur Institute's T cell lines, frozen in liquid nitrogen at −346°F (−210°C). Leibowitch was angry with the Pasteur Institute for turning him down for a job. To undermine the team at Pasteur, he wanted to help Gallo prove that HTLV, not BRU, was the cause of AIDS. Leibowitch gave Gallo the French T cell lines to assist with this work.

SEARCHING FOR A LINK

By March 1983, Robert Gallo was working on an article for *Science* that would describe the link he saw between HTLV and AIDS. The article would be published on May 20, the same day Gallo planned to hold a press conference announcing the discovery.

Gallo needed concrete examples to prove his theory, but he had major problems finding any. His lab had meticulously examined blood from nearly one hundred U.S. AIDS patients, but only two samples tested positive for HTLV. This was not enough to prove a connection between HTLV and AIDS.

Gallo's research took an unexpected turn when he began studying the T cell lines from French AIDS patients provided by Leibowitch. Two of the French T cell lines tested positive for HTLV. With the U.S. and French blood samples, Gallo now had four samples from AIDS patients that tested positive for HTLV. However, four HTLV cases out of a hundred samples did not provide enough solid scientific evidence of an HTLV-AIDS connection.

Robert Gallo *(second from left)* discusses AIDS research with colleagues in the early 1980s.

TRACKING
THE PATH OF HIV

When AIDS became a central focus for doctors in the 1980s, researchers began combing through medical records to track the path of the disease and to search for its origins. Studies led researchers to conclude that the AIDS virus is closely related to simian immunodeficiency virus, or SIV. The word *simian* refers to a group of animals that includes monkeys, apes, and humans.

Researchers think SIV jumped from monkeys to humans sometime between 1884 and 1924. According to the "hunter theory," an unknown African hunter got SIV when he was bitten by a chimpanzee or when he cut himself while butchering a chimpanzee. Once the virus was in the hunter's bloodstream, it mutated (changed) into a human virus.

From the infected hunter, the virus spread to other people in Africa and eventually beyond Africa. A fifteen-year-old boy known only as Robert R., from Saint Louis, Missouri, is the first North American known to have died from AIDS. He was a male prostitute and probably contracted the disease through sex with another man. He died in 1969.

THE NEW HUMAN LENTIVIRUS

Back in France, Montagnier was getting closer to linking BRU to AIDS. In April 1983, he had a breakthrough. He learned of a type of slow-acting retrovirus known as a lentivirus. Lentiviruses have a long incubation period—the time between infection and the onset of illness. That means they remain inactive in blood cells for a long time before bursting into activity and spreading rapidly throughout the body. Montagnier did research on equine anemia virus, a lentivirus found in horses. He discovered it was very similar to the BRU retrovirus in AIDS patients.

Although he could not conclusively link the BRU virus to AIDS, Montagnier decided to write an article for *Science* describing BRU as a new human lentivirus. The article summarized his findings about BRU in ARC patient Frédéric Brugière.

As a professional courtesy, Montagnier asked Robert Gallo to read the article before publication. This proved to be a mistake, according to Montagnier:

> *In my haste, I forgot to write a summary that was to be published at the head of the article. Gallo offered to write it for me. I accepted, just to save time. His summary, however, implied that our virus should be included in the family of HTLV viruses, whereas the rest of the article . . . indicated the contrary. Indeed, we were already engaged, without our knowing it, in a scientific quarrel that would not be settled for a number of years.*

> "We were already engaged, without our knowing it, in a scientific quarrel that would not be settled for a number of years."
>
> —Luc Montagnier, 1999

BRU BECOMES LAV

The summary at the head of a scientific article was crucial. At this time of limited computer memory, the summary of an article was the only part entered into medical databases. Therefore, when scientists used databases for research, they saw only summaries. The summary that Gallo wrote for Montagnier's article left the impression that the BRU lentivirus and HTLV were one and the same. In addition, Gallo's article on the suspected link between HTLV and AIDS appeared in the same issue of *Science* (May 20) as Montagnier's article. But Gallo's piece appeared on the first pages of the magazine, with Montagnier's article on later pages. This placement gave many readers the impression that Montagnier's paper was simply confirming the work done by the Americans. After the articles were published, the mainstream press largely ignored Montagnier's work and printed dozens of stories linking HTLV to AIDS.

Montagnier's disappointment with the misinformation made him work harder. In June 1983, he announced that the new lentivirus had been found in at least four patients with ARC. Because Frédéric Brugière, from whom the virus had first come, had lymphadenopathy (persistent swollen lymph glands), Montagnier changed the name from BRU to lymphadenopathy-associated virus, or LAV. Montagnier wrote that "LAV was closely related to . . . lentiviruses and only distantly related to HTLV."

Françoise Brun-Vezinet knew of a simple blood test called an enzyme-linked immunosorbent assay (ELISA), which could be used to detect various diseases. The test uses a tiny piece of a virus to attract blood-borne antibodies specific to that virus. Brun-Vezinet used a tiny piece of LAV

This microscopic photograph shows lymphadenopathy-associated virus, or LAV, the French name for the AIDS virus.

to create a LAV-based ELISA test. With this test, technicians could analyze a blood sample from a patient. If the blood sample changed color during testing, LAV antibodies were present, meaning the patient had LAV.

From July through August, Brun-Vezinet tested blood samples from ARC and AIDS patients in Europe, Haiti, and Africa. She used her ELISA test to detect LAV and used other methods to detect the presence of HTLV. While only 15 percent of ARC patients had HTLV, more than 75 percent tested positive for LAV. But Brun-Vezinet was so busy with her work that she did not write about her findings.

Although nothing had been published about the ELISA/LAV work, Gallo knew what the French researchers were doing. He asked Luc Montagnier for LAV blood samples and for antibodies taken from Frédéric Brugière. Montagnier hand delivered the samples to Gallo on a trip to the National Institutes of Health on July 17.

SHOWDOWN IN COLD SPRING HARBOR

By September the team at the Pasteur Institute was able to show a fundamental link between LAV and AIDS. However, when Montagnier and Gallo spoke at a meeting in Cold Spring Harbor, New York, on September 15, 1983, the two men clashed. The Cold Spring Harbor gathering was a meeting of the world's top virologists, and almost all were convinced of Gallo's theory that HTLV caused AIDS. In fact, Montagnier described the meeting as a "festival of HTLV."

Montagnier was scheduled to give a lecture about the Pasteur Institute's LAV research, but he was given only twenty minutes to speak at the very end of the proceedings. When he told the small audience, which included Gallo, that LAV was not related to HTLV, some scientists laughed out loud.

After the meeting, Montagnier informed Gallo that Brun-Vezinet had applied for a European patent (the legal right to make, use, and sell something) for the LAV blood test that very morning. Gallo became angry. He said the patent was a bad idea, because to his knowledge LAV was not the cause of AIDS. Gallo also hinted that T cell lines at the Pasteur Institute had been contaminated with equine lentivirus, leading to inaccurate test results.

Despite his anger, Gallo seemed to believe the French findings had some merit—although he didn't admit it in public. Gallo needed more LAV cell lines so he could continue his research. So before Montagnier left Cold Spring Harbor, Gallo slipped him a hastily scribbled note, asking for another shipment of LAV.

"WE WERE WRONG"

When Montagnier returned to Paris after the Cold Spring Harbor meeting, he tried to publish an article linking LAV to AIDS, but the major scientific journals turned him down. Montagnier believed the publishers were waiting for Gallo to prove the HTLV-AIDS connection and were not interested in conflicting theories.

But Mikulas Popovic, a virologist at the National Institutes of Health, had heard Montagnier's lecture in Cold Spring Harbor and thought it made sense. Popovic started growing T cell lines with the LAV blood samples that Gallo had received from Montagnier the previous July.

Popovic also studied cells from ten AIDS and ARC patients. While three tested positive for HTLV, all ten tested positive for LAV. Popovic suddenly understood Gallo's problem. Because Gallo believed that HTLV caused AIDS, he had spent more than a year looking for HTLV antibodies in blood samples. Because he was looking for HTLV, he focused only on that virus. He had not looked for LAV because he did not believe it was the source of the problem. Popovic later gave credit to the French researchers: "I came to the conclusion that we were wrong [about HTLV], and Barré-Sinoussi was right."[

About a week after the Cold Spring Harbor meeting, the Pasteur Institute shipped the blood samples Gallo had requested from Montagnier. Gallo was not in the lab when the package arrived, but it came with an agreement that limited the samples to AIDS research only. They could not be used for any industrial or commercial purpose without the prior written consent of the director of the Pasteur Institute. Popovic barely glanced at the document, signed it, and dated it September 23, 1983.

With the new blood samples, Popovic began searching for a way to grow

LAV T cell lines without using injections of T cell growth factor. This was a difficult process. With immortalized T cell lines, he could develop a new test for the presence of the AIDS virus in blood samples. The trick would be generating T cells faster than LAV could kill them. Popovic solved the problem by combining samples from ten different patients with slightly different strains of LAV. This gave him a higher chance that one of the LAV strains would allow T cells to survive. The method was controversial because Popovic could not identify the one strain out of ten that worked best. However, it did allow him to grow immortalized LAV T cell lines. Because his technique was not considered proper science, Popovic initially kept this development to himself. No one knows exactly when Popovic informed Gallo of his discovery.

By December 1983, researchers at NCI in Bethesda, Maryland, had received substantial quantities of LAV from the Pasteur Institute. Based on Popovic's studies, Gallo and the other U.S. researchers realized that LAV and HTLV were completely different in genetic makeup. However, this information remained confidential, and Montagnier and his team did not learn of these developments.

Meanwhile, on December 5, the Pasteur Institute applied for a U.S. patent on its LAV blood test. It also worked with a shipment of thirty blood samples taken from men in San Francisco. Ten samples were from gay men with AIDS, ten were from gay men with persistent swollen glands (lymphadenopathy), and ten were from heterosexuals who were not at risk for AIDS. The samples were blind, meaning they were marked only with code numbers. By looking for LAV antibodies, the French were able to successfully identify the twenty samples taken from men with AIDS or with swollen glands and the ten samples taken from the men with no risk for AIDS.

AN INDISPUTABLE LINK

By January 1984, the Pasteur Institute team was clarifying the genetic configurations of LAV and HTLV. In addition, French researchers had isolated the first LAV samples from a hemophiliac. This meticulous research was carefully compiled into scientific papers written by Brun-Vezinet, Montagnier,

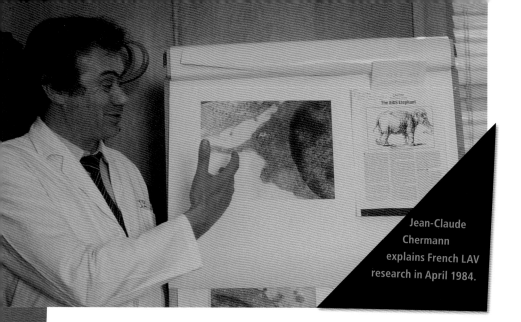

and other researchers at the Pasteur Institute. However, the French researchers were unsure when or if the articles would be published.

On February 7, 1984, French researcher Jean-Claude Chermann traveled to Park City, Utah, to present his findings at a meeting of 150 AIDS researchers organized by UCLA. In halting English, Chermann explained in great detail the research conducted at the Pasteur Institute that proved an indisputable link between LAV and AIDS.

Gallo, who also attended the meeting, turned pale. In a question-and-answer session after Chermann's speech, he accused the French of working with contaminated viruses. Gallo also demanded that LAV be called HTLV-3 (an unrelated retrovirus called HTLV-2 had been discovered in 1981). Chermann held his ground and repeatedly stated that LAV was not related to HTLV.

About a week later, Chermann spoke to a group of researchers and top executives at the CDC, convincing most of them that LAV, not HTLV, caused AIDS. Walter Dowdle, who ran the CDC's Center for Infectious Diseases, was critical of Gallo: "We came away convinced that [the French] had the agent [the virus that caused AIDS]. . . . We didn't know what was happening in Gallo's lab. We only knew he was working on something. . . . There was no real way to compare what was going on in both labs."

WARRING SUPERPOWERS

The news of the French discovery traveled up the chain of command at the Department of Health and Human Services, which oversees the CDC and the National Institutes of Health. Margaret Heckler, secretary of HHS, learned that the cause of AIDS—which she called the nation's most urgent health priority—had been found not in Bethesda but in Paris.

Don Francis, a retrovirologist at the CDC, wanted to make a joint announcement with the CDC, NCI, and Pasteur Institute about the French discovery of LAV. Francis believed that an agreement between the U.S. and French institutions was necessary for the scientific community to move on in the search for a cure for AIDS.

> "Don't panic if I get attention. And I'm going to get attention."
>
> Robert Gallo to Luc Montagnier and his team of French AIDS researchers, 1984

Yet while French scientists had been linking LAV to AIDS for more than a year, Robert Gallo refused to accept that he had been wrong all along. Furthermore, Gallo would not share details about his discovery of the virus he called HTLV-3. He said that HTLV-3 might not even be related to LAV. Gallo then made bold plans to hold a press conference and to publish an article in *Science* announcing his discovery of the AIDS virus.

Montagnier, Chermann, Barré-Sinoussi, and the other French scientists were furious. Gallo reassured the French team that they would get credit for their work—eventually. He told them, "Look, one thing. Don't panic if I get attention. And I'm going to get attention. Don't panic. A month later we'll come back and make a joint announcement. I'll analyze your virus and we'll go together."

CHAPTER FIVE

DISPUTES AND
LAWSUITS

With AIDS patients dying by the hundreds, the pressing medical goal on both sides of the Atlantic was to invent a blood test that would identify patients who had the AIDS virus.

Both sides also knew that vast amounts of money were at stake as well. An AIDS test kit was expected to generate millions of dollars in profits each year. It seemed as if the French had won the race.

On December 5, 1983, the Pasteur Institute, which had already applied for a European patent for the LAV test, applied for a U.S. patent. The U.S. patent would be necessary if the Pasteur Institute wanted to sell the test in the United States. If approved by the U.S. Patent and Trademark Office (PTO), the patent would give the Pasteur Institute the exclusive right to profit from this breakthrough test in the lucrative U.S. market. But the approval of a medical patent is a complex, time-consuming process that can take years to complete. To ensure that a product is safe and effective, the U.S. Food and Drug Administration (FDA) tests and retests it and conducts trials on volunteers.

While the Pasteur Institute patent process was just beginning, the question over who had discovered the AIDS virus was coming to a head. On April 22, 1984, James Mason, director of the CDC, told the *New York Times*," I believe [researchers have discovered] the cause of AIDS, and it is an exciting discovery. The public needs to know that this is a breakthrough and that it is significant." The article went on to report that the cause of AIDS was LAV, isolated by Luc Montagnier and his colleagues in France. However, the next day, Mason's comments were all but forgotten when HHS secretary Margaret Heckler announced that Robert Gallo had isolated the AIDS virus in his lab in the United States.

> "Today we add another miracle to the long honor roll of American science. Today's discovery represents a triumph of science over a dreaded disease [AIDS]."
>
> HHS secretary Margaret Heckler, April 23, 1984, announcing the discovery of the AIDS virus by Robert Gallo and his team

CLAIMING CREDIT

On April 23, 1984, Heckler stood before an eager press conference audience in Washington, D.C., and said, "Today we add another miracle to the long honor roll of American science. Today's discovery represents a triumph of science over a dreaded disease [AIDS]."

Heckler went on to say that U.S. scientists had found the AIDS virus, called HTLV-3, and that HHS had applied for a patent on an HTLV-3 ELISA test. She said the test would be 100 percent accurate and available within six months. The test would allow two stunning breakthroughs. First, it would allow blood banks to screen blood, ensuring that blood used in transfusions was free from the AIDS virus. The test would also allow doctors to promptly diagnose those with the disease, helping to prevent its spread. Heckler also noted that Robert Gallo had developed a way to produce great quantities of the AIDS virus, which would be needed for testing blood used in transfusions. Luc Montagnier's name never even came up.

"A BITTER TASTE"

Heckler's announcement left the French feeling cheated. Years later, when Montagnier recalled the Washington, D.C., press conference in his 1999 autobiography, he wrote, "Even after fifteen years these events leave a bitter taste in my mouth." Randy Shilts, a renowned U.S. author on the history of AIDS, wrote, "The U.S. government had taken a sleazy path, claiming credit for something that had been done by others a year before."

Yet as criticisms arose, Gallo and other officials at the NCI dismissed them. They did not feel the French deserved equal credit for the AIDS test. Not only had Gallo done more initial work to isolate retroviruses, the Americans argued, but Popovic had developed the method for the mass production of HTLV-3 cells for use in test kits.

The transatlantic rivalry intensified when articles by Gallo about HTLV-3 appeared in the May 4, 1984, issue of *Science*. The stories were announced with the headline "Strong New Candidate for AIDS Agent [virus]." In four separate articles, Gallo explained that researchers at NCI had isolated HTLV-3 from forty-eight patients and had created immortalized T cell lines of the virus.

The articles were accompanied by eight pictures taken with electron microscopes. The pictures showed three viruses in various stages of development. The first series of pictures, two each of HTLV-1 and HTLV-2, showed the similarities between the viruses. The third series contained four images labeled HTLV-3, but they were actually pictures of LAV that Montagnier had sent Gallo the previous year. Without usable photos of HTLV-3 of his own, Gallo had knowingly mislabeled Montagnier's photos, claiming credit for them himself.

RACING FOR A GENE MAP

At the Heckler press conference, Gallo had promised to provide a sample of HTLV-3 to the Pasteur Institute so it could be compared to LAV. On May 15, Gallo sent the sample to Paris with researcher M. G. Sarngadharan, nicknamed Sarang. After working for four days, Sarang and Jean-Claude Chermann concluded that the proteins in HTLV-3 and LAV were the same sizes and weights. Gallo was informed that the two viruses were nearly identical.

Gallo disputed this claim. Speaking on the telephone, he told Montagnier that the LAV samples the French were using had been contaminated by the HTLV-3 provided by Sarang. Gallo later wrote that Montagnier had no reaction to this statement. However, according to Montagnier, "If we had used videophones, he would have seen me literally leap out of my chair, on the very edge of apoplexy [a fit of anger]." Montagnier countered Gallo's charge, saying that if there was any contamination, it had been at Gallo's lab. Montagnier later recalled, "I began to seriously ask myself whether HTLV-3 was not merely another name for LAV."

Luc Montagnier holds two images in 1984. The top picture shows HTLV, discovered by Robert Gallo. The bottom image shows Montagnier's discovery: LAV.

To solve the question of whether or not the viruses were the same, the French and Americans began a race to map the genetic code of the two viruses. This complex and difficult process involves studying and comparing the nine thousand sequences of genes that make up the genetic code in the DNA and RNA of the viruses.

By November 1984, a team of French researchers had made a map of the nine thousand LAV genes, labeled with a complicated system using letters of the alphabet. Meanwhile, Gallo assigned a team of nineteen researchers in Bethesda, who worked night and day for more than three months to map HTLV-3.

On December 6, as the work at Bethesda was winding up, Simon Wain-Hobson, a representative of the Pasteur Institute, presented Gallo with the first gene map of LAV. It was immediately clear to the U.S. research team that the DNA maps of HTLV-3 and LAV were the same.

The two teams raced to publish their gene maps in the influential journal *Nature*. Like most scientific journals, *Nature* had a first-come, first-published policy—so it was important to beat the other team with an article. Gallo submitted his DNA map of HTLV-3 to the magazine a few days before the French team submitted its map. His pictures of the retrovirus appeared in the January 23, 1985, issue.

FALSE POSITIVES

By February 1985, the FDA was close to licensing Gallo's HTLV-3 blood test. But in fact, Gallo's test was inaccurate. FDA trials showed that 60 percent of blood samples without the AIDS virus wrongly tested positive for the disease. (A test result that wrongly shows the presence of a disease is known as a false positive.) The Pasteur Institute LAV test was more accurate. Yet it was still waiting for FDA approval, even though the French test had been submitted much earlier than Gallo's.

Many observers viewed the fast-track approval of the U.S. test as a political necessity. Secretary Heckler had promised the public an AIDS blood test by October 1984, and by early 1985, it was still not available. The FDA was under intense pressure to approve the test to maintain Heckler's credibility, along with that of the HHS.

On March 2, the FDA approved the HTLV-3 blood test, to be manufactured by Illinois-based Abbott Laboratories. The first test kits were released in Chicago, at a blood bank near Abbott's headquarters. The test kits were accompanied by a warning that said false positive test results could be expected.

By April 1985, three million test kits had been distributed to check the U.S. blood supply. Even allowing for false positives, the tests helped identify massive amounts of AIDS-infected blood. By withdrawing this blood from circulation, health professionals were able to stop the spread of the virus through transfusions.

"JUST PLAIN PRESSURE"

After the FDA approved their AIDS test kit, Robert Gallo and the HHS were awarded a U.S. patent for the test on May 28, 1985. The HHS would get a 5 percent royalty (share of the profits) from the test—about $5 million annually. In addition, for their part in developing the test, Gallo and Popovic would earn about $100,000 a year each.

But after the approval, Gallo wrote, "from all sides and in big doses, came [law]suits over royalties to the blood test, lawyers, media, politics and just plain pressure." The pressure began on August 6, when Raymond Dedonder, director of the Pasteur Institute, traveled to Washington, D.C., accompanied by four lawyers. He had come to protest the FDA's delay in licensing the LAV blood test. Dedonder pointed out that the French had applied for the blood test patent in December 1983, five months before the HHS had.

"[It is] a well-established fact that the virus responsible for AIDS has been discovered by the group working at the Pasteur Institute. This is supported by competent scientists all over the world," Dedonder said. The French wanted the U.S. government to revoke the U.S. patent and give it to the Pasteur Institute instead.

> "[It is] a well-established fact that the virus responsible for AIDS has been discovered by the group working at the Pasteur Institute. This is supported by competent scientists all over the world."
>
> **Raymond Dedonder, director of the Pasteur Institute, contesting HHS's claim that U.S. scientists discovered the AIDS virus, 1985**

How HIV Reproduces

T cell

1. An HIV particle meets a T cell. The knobby protein key on HIV's outer coat fits snugly into the T cell's receptor site. Attachment begins.

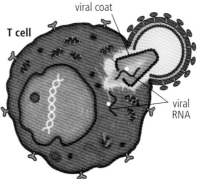

outer coat

receptor site

T cell nucleus

outer coat

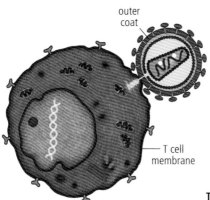

2. HIV's outer coat fuses with the outside membrane of the T cell.

T cell membrane

viral coat

T cell

3. Once inside the T cell, the virus sheds its coat. Two strands of RNA are released into the T cell.

viral RNA

reverse transcriptase

viral RNA

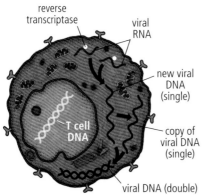

new viral DNA (single)

T cell DNA

copy of viral DNA (single)

viral DNA (double)

4. Reverse transcriptase copies a single strand of DNA from the two strands of viral RNA. RNAse chops off the old RNA from the DNA copy. Then polymerase makes another exact copy of the new viral DNA and links the strands of DNA.

5. The brand-new double strand of viral DNA moves into the nucleus of the T cell. Once inside, integrase fuses the viral DNA with the T cell's DNA. Hijacking is complete.

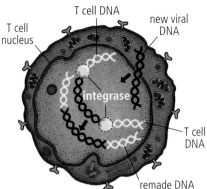

6. The remade DNA begins issuing orders for the production of proteins necessary to build new HIV particles. Using instructions in the form of messenger RNA and transfer RNA, ribosomes in the T cell begin assembling amino acids into large, inactive proteins. These proteins move to the cell membrane.

7. At the membrane, the HIV particles are released from the T cell by a process called budding. The young HIV particles are not infectious.

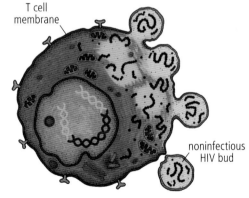

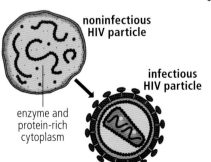

8. Protease molecules split the large proteins inside the HIV particle into a bunch of smaller proteins and enzymes. With that, the HIV particle is a mature, infectious retrovirus.

Another part of the dispute concerned the document casually signed by Popovic on September 23, 1983, when he received a LAV delivery from the Pasteur Institute. The document stated that the LAV was for research only and could not be used for industrial or commercial purposes. The French accused HHS of breach of contract, charging that the Americans had used French LAV to develop the U.S. blood test.

In his defense, Gallo countered that the LAV samples sent to Bethesda in 1983 were too small for growing the large batches of virus cell lines needed to produce a blood test. Gallo stated that HTLV-3 had been used to grow the virus, ignoring that Popovic had originally used French LAV.

Negotiations between lawyers and officials from both sides dragged on for months. Lawyers reviewed scientific paperwork from the U.S. labs and the French labs. The French had kept meticulous records of their experiments in dozens of hardbound notebooks. The labs in Bethesda, however, had no such records. When investigators attempted to review Popovic's work, they found nearly unreadable scraps of paper stuffed into drawers. The most notable gap in the record keeping concerned Popovic's work with the LAV samples sent from the Pasteur Institute in 1983—the samples that allowed him to grow LAV T cell lines.

"DISSERVICE TO THE DISCOVERERS"

The HHS maintained that there was nothing to support the claims that Gallo had used French LAV to make his blood test. When no settlement could be reached, on December 12, 1985, the Pasteur Institute filed a lawsuit against the U.S. government. The suit charged that the Gallo blood test was being manufactured using LAV discovered in France. The Pasteur Institute believed that it—not HHS—deserved the millions of dollars in royalties as well as recognition for the discovery of the AIDS virus.

On February 19, 1986, while the two sides were preparing their court cases, the FDA finally licensed the Pasteur Institute's AIDS test for sale in the United States. It would be manufactured by Seattle-based Genetic Systems.

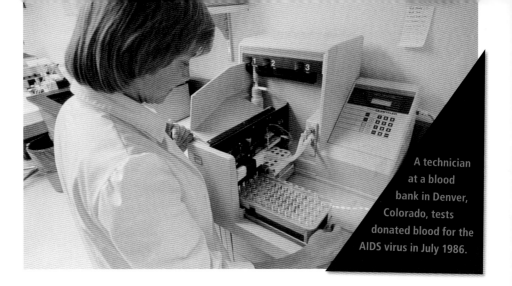

A technician at a blood bank in Denver, Colorado, tests donated blood for the AIDS virus in July 1986.

However, the test still had not received a patent from the PTO. In addition, the FDA described the Pasteur Institute test as a test for HTLV-3. Dedonder wrote a letter to the FDA in protest. He said:

The FDA knows perfectly well that the Genetic Systems kit works with LAV, the virus isolated by the Pasteur Group in January, 1983, more than one year before the description of HTLV-3 by Gallo and his co-workers. . . . [This designation] is wrong, both historically and scientifically and does a disservice to the discoverers of the AIDS virus [Montagnier and others], who...are apparently not to be allowed the ordinary right to see in everyday use, on their own product, the name they chose for the AIDS virus.

Meanwhile, fear of AIDS and prejudice against gay people were very high, and false positives from the Abbott AIDS test were taking a terrible toll. For example, some employers fired people who tested positive for AIDS. Some people divorced spouses who tested positive. Those who tested positive experienced much of the trauma associated with contracting a fatal disease—even if they didn't really have it. The problem was so severe that the Red Cross, which operates blood banks around the world, largely switched from the Abbott test to the more reliable French test made by Genetic Systems.

CHAPTER SIX

IN THE
MUD

By 1986 the debate over who had discovered the AIDS virus and who owned the rights to the AIDS blood test was being fought in courtrooms.

Another dispute had erupted over naming the AIDS virus. In the field of microbiology, whoever discovers a virus has the right to name it. Because Robert Gallo insisted that he had discovered the AIDS virus, he called it HTLV-3. Luc Montagnier continued to use his name, LAV.

To settle this dispute, scientists set up a fourteen-member international naming committee, chaired by Harold Varmus, an expert in avian (bird) retroviruses. As soon as the committee was formed, Gallo sent Varmus a twenty-point document arguing for HTLV-3 as the fair and accurate name for the AIDS virus.

In the end, the Varmus committee didn't choose either name. In May 1986, the committee decided the AIDS virus would be named human immunodeficiency virus, or HIV. Luc Montagnier supported this decision.

Gallo, refusing to gracefully accept defeat, continued to write articles using the term *HTLV-3*.

Gallo did make some concessions to his rival. In April 1986, he publicly admitted that he had used Pasteur Institute images of HTLV-3 for his May 1984 *Science* article without labeling or crediting them correctly. Yet he insisted he had isolated the AIDS virus in late 1982, three months before the French reported isolating LAV.

"A SELF-SERVING DISPUTE"

The French lawsuit, *Pasteur Institute v the United States,* was heard by the U.S. Claims Court in Washington, D.C., in September 1986. In patent law, the date a product is first successfully used is considered the date of its invention. With the AIDS test, this was the date the ELISA was first used to test blood samples for AIDS antibodies. For Gallo to be triumphant in this case, the HHS lawyers would have to convince the court that the Americans had used their test first. Yet the French clearly had the winning claim. They had documented evidence that they had used their test before the Americans. So HHS lawyers tried instead to argue that the two tests were completely different inventions, which they were not.

With a weak argument, HHS lawyers came up with other legal methods to tie up the case in court. They hoped the French would tire of the fight and agree to a settlement in Gallo's favor. However, independent scientists watching the bitter dispute did not think a courtroom was the place to settle complex matters of scientific research. They felt the lawsuit was an embarrassment to the scientific community and would hold up progress in the fight against AIDS. So in November 1986, days after Ronald Reagan was elected to a second term as U.S. president, nine Nobel Prize winners made an appeal to him. They asked the president to personally intervene and resolve the case as quickly as possible. They wrote, "Given the grave crisis which AIDS presents, it does not befit the scientific community to be engaged in what appears to be a self-serving dispute." The president did not respond to the letter.

SALK TO THE RESCUE

Then a surprising mediator entered the fray. Virologist Jonas Salk had developed the first safe and effective polio vaccine in 1955. He had become a worldwide celebrity for helping stop a polio epidemic that killed thousands of people each year and left hundreds of thousands, many of them children, severely disabled. Like Gallo and Montagnier, Salk had experienced his own bitter rivalry, in his case with researcher Albert Sabin, over who deserved credit for stamping out polio. And like Gallo, Salk had been accused of taking credit for the work of other people.

> "Professor Gallo has not told the truth."
>
> Luc Montagnier, commenting on the Office of Scientific Integrity investigations of Robert Gallo, 1991

To help mediate the AIDS virus dispute, Salk went to HHS lawyers and made a proposal. The French would be granted their patent and allowed to sell their test, while Abbott would be allowed to continue marketing the Gallo test. Profits from the two tests would be paid to a joint foundation overseen by directors of the HHS and the Pasteur Institute. One-third of the royalties would go to HHS, one-third to Pasteur, and one-third to an organization

Jonas Salk—who became famous for developing the first polio vaccine—mediated an agreement between the HHS and the Pasteur Institute. Here he attends an AIDS conference in Canada in 1989.

called the World AIDS Foundation, created to fund AIDS research projects in poor nations. Salk also proposed that Gallo and Montagnier share credit for discovering the AIDS virus and coauthor an official history about the discovery of HIV. The two sides agreed to the basics of the proposal. The settlement was announced publicly on March 31, 1987, at a White House Rose Garden ceremony attended by President Reagan and French president Jacques Chirac.

"A DOUBLE FRAUD"

The settlement ended the battle over patents and royalties. But the issue of who had discovered HIV and when was far from resolved. Only eight days after presidents Reagan and Chirac appeared in the Rose Garden, a scientist working at the Los Alamos National Laboratory in New Mexico announced a startling discovery. Gerald Myers, a leading HIV genetic analyst, had conducted a thorough investigation of the French and U.S. AIDS viruses named in the patents. Because of his expertise, Myers could decipher incredibly complex DNA sequences and determine their genetic heritage. During the course of his work, he had compiled the evolution of the AIDS virus in Africa, tracing the infection from apes to human beings.

Myers determined that the HTLV-3 and LAV samples were not only genetically similar, but they had come from the same patient. This meant the two viruses could not have been discovered independently. Myers continued to study the viruses and confirmed that the HTLV-3 sample owned by Gallo had undoubtedly come from the Pasteur Institute's LAV.

Myers informed U.S. officials of his discovery. He sent letters to several NIH and NCI scientists and senior scientific administrators, including Robert Gallo. Myers said a "double fraud" had been perpetrated on the scientific community. The first fraud was Gallo declaring HTLV-3 to be different from LAV. The second fraud was Gallo's insistence that he had not used French LAV to develop his blood test. In response to the letter, Gallo and his team maintained an official silence.

DIGGING DEEPER

But John Crewdson, an investigative reporter with the *Chicago Tribune,* wanted to know more. He began to look carefully into the fraud charges. On November 19, 1989, the *Chicago Tribune* published the results of Crewdson's investigation—a sixteen-page story. It concluded that Gallo had indeed committed fraud when he claimed that Pasteur's LAV was his HTLV-3.

Crewdson's article—with its dramatic confirmation of unprofessional behavior by a prominent scientist—led to several official investigations by the NIH Office of Scientific Integrity (OSI). The NIH maintains its credibility by ensuring the utmost reliability among its top-notch scientists. It takes charges against researchers extremely seriously. Yet during the course of this inquiry, Gallo exhibited a defiant attitude, telling OSI investigators the following:

> **I'm interested in a vaccine and in curing the disease. I'm interested in basic science and how the virus works. Do you think I'm going to get back there in the mud of whether [HTLV–3] and LAV came from this lab or the other lab . . . ? I mean, who . . . cared?**

When information about the NIH investigation became public in May 1991, Luc Montagnier called a press conference. He told reporters, "Professor Gallo has not told the truth." Embroiled in a controversy that wouldn't go away, Gallo finally tried to defend himself. He wrote in *Nature* that LAV samples had accidentally contaminated virus cultures in his laboratory and claimed he had been unaware of the problem. The investigators determined otherwise.

In 1992 the OSI was merged into a new agency, the Office of Research Integrity (ORI), which continued the investigation. In December, after a nearly three-year inquiry, the ORI concluded that Gallo had committed scientific misconduct by falsely reporting in the May 1984 issue of *Science* that he had isolated the AIDS virus. The report went on to say that Gallo had intentionally misled his colleagues to get credit for the discovery while diminishing the credit due to researchers at the Pasteur Institute. Even more devastating, the report pointed out that Gallo's self-serving actions had "impeded potential AIDS research progress" by diverting scientists from the successful work conducted by the French team.

The ORI ruling did not stand, however. Gallo and Popovic appealed the ruling to a special panel within the ORI. The panel, made up of lawyers, not scientists, established a new definition of scientific misconduct, as well as a new and extremely difficult standard for proving misconduct. The panel ruled that for a scientist to be guilty of misconduct, he or she had to have deliberately intended to deceive others and that any false statements made by the scientist had to have a significant effect on research conclusions, with no possibility of honest error. Because the ORI could not prove that Gallo's misbehavior was deliberate, on November 12, 1993, the ORI withdrew its decision that Gallo and Popovic had committed scientific misconduct.

But Gallo was not in the clear yet. The ORI report touched off another investigation—this one by the U.S. House of Representatives Subcommittee on Oversight and Investigations. This committee was chaired by congressional representative John Dingell, a Democrat from Michigan. In late 1994, the Dingell investigation resulted in a 336-page report. It stated clearly that HHS officials had been involved in a cover-up, lying about the role played by U.S. scientists in the discovery of the AIDS virus and the invention of the AIDS test. The House of Representatives never officially recognized the Dingell report, however, because it criticized the Republican Reagan administration for its role in the cover-up. Led by a majority of Republicans, the House was unwilling to put its weight behind the report.

"Do you think I'm going to get back there in the mud of whether [HTLV–3] and LAV came from this lab or the other lab when I have all kinds of other [viruses] and things are moving like a bullet?... I mean, who... cared?"

Robert Gallo to OSI investigators, 1990

FROM ADVERSARIES TO ALLIES

When HIV/AIDS first became a public health crisis in the early 1980s, the work of Robert Gallo and Luc Montagnier led to rapid, unprecedented scientific discoveries.

Between 1983 and 1985, the scientists and their colleagues isolated the AIDS virus, learned about its modes of transmission, and mapped its genes.

This work led to lifesaving advancements in treating patients with HIV/AIDS. In 1985 scientists at NCI, working with the pharmaceutical company GlaxoSmithKline, developed an antiretroviral drug called azidothymidine (AZT). The drug interferes with RT and slows the spread of HIV. The FDA approved AZT for the treatment of HIV/AIDS patients in March 1987. AZT has unpleasant side effects, such as severe nausea. But the drug and other antiretroviral drugs that followed it have prolonged the lives of many AIDS patients—sometimes by many years.

As AIDS research moved forward, Robert Gallo and Luc Montagnier put their intense rivalry to rest. In 2002 the two pioneering scientists became codirectors of the Program for International Viral Collaboration. This organization works to speed discovery of an AIDS vaccine.

In 2008 Luc Montagnier received a great and long overdue honor. He and researcher Françoise Barré-Sinoussi won the Nobel Prize in Medicine for their work in isolating HIV. The following year, on the twenty-fifth anniversary of the isolation of HIV, Gallo and Montagnier teamed up again to issue a Global Call to Action to stop the spread of AIDS. This platform included a call for more education about AIDS prevention, more AIDS treatment in poor nations, and continued research into vaccines and other new treatments for AIDS.

By 2011 more than 34 million people worldwide were living with HIV/AIDS. Almost three million people were newly infected with HIV in 2010. Nearly two million people died of AIDS that year. These numbers show that HIV/AIDS is still a devastating global killer.

At the same time, scientists continue to make strides in the fight against AIDS. For instance, in 2011 researchers discovered that HIV-infected people could reduce transmission to noninfected people by taking antiretroviral drugs and that noninfected people could also reduce their risk of infection by taking antiretrovirals. But despite impressive scientific advancements, Luc Montagnier offers these cautions:

> *Even though we know very well the molecular biology of this virus, we still know little about how it is transmitted, why antiretroviral treatment cannot get rid of it completely, and so on. There are still basic questions to answer, and at the same time we have to save the lives of patients and try to reduce the duration of treatment. I think this is key if we are to beat this disease in the twenty-first century. I hope I will see that during my lifetime.*

TIMELINE

1969 A fifteen-year-old-boy, known only as Robert R., dies in Saint Louis, Missouri. He is the first North American known to have died of AIDS.

1971 Virologist Robert Gallo begins research to find a human retrovirus.

1979 - 1980 Doctors in the United States and Europe begin seeing a rise in the number of patients with mysterious ailments related to a breakdown of the body's immune system.

1981 Robert Gallo and his colleagues find a retrovirus that causes a type of leukemia in humans. They name it human T-cell leukemia virus (HTLV). The Centers for Disease Control and Prevention (CDC) publishes the first official report on what will become known as the AIDS epidemic.

1982 The CDC coins the name acquired immunodeficiency syndrome, or AIDS, for the immune system disease. French doctors set up a task force to study AIDS.

1983 January: Researchers at the Pasteur Institute in Paris, France, isolate a human retrovirus, which they name BRU.

May: French virologist Luc Montagnier writes an article for the journal *Science* describing BRU, which he identifies as a slow-growing lentivirus. Robert Gallo writes the summary for the article, in which he incorrectly describes BRU as a form of HTLV.

June: Luc Montagnier changes the name BRU to lymphadenopathy-associated virus (LAV) because people with the virus have lymphadenopathy, or persistent swollen lymph glands.

July: French medical technician Françoise Brun develops a blood test for detecting LAV. Luc Montagnier delivers LAV blood samples to Robert Gallo at the National Cancer Institute in Maryland.

September: Robert Gallo and Luc Montagnier make presentations at a meeting of virologists at Cold Spring Harbor, New York. Gallo tells the group that HTLV causes AIDS. Montagnier, on the other hand, says that LAV causes AIDS. The two men have a heated personal exchange about their competing theories.

October: National Institutes of Health researcher Mikulas Popovic develops immortalized LAV T cell lines using LAV samples from the Pasteur Institute. The cell lines give researchers large amounts of T cells for further study.

December: The Pasteur Institute applies for a U.S. patent on its LAV blood test.

1984 February: French virologist Jean-Claude Chermann presents details of the Pasteur Institute's work on LAV to a meeting of AIDS researchers in Utah.

March: French scientists report finding LAV in about 90 percent of patients with AIDS and AIDS-related complex.

April: Health and Human Services (HHS) secretary Margaret Heckler announces that Robert Gallo has discovered the probable cause of AIDS, a retrovirus called HTLV-3. The HHS applies for a patent on an HTLV-3 ELISA test.

Science publishes four articles by Robert Gallo about his work with HTLV-3. The articles include pictures of LAV provided by Luc Montagnier but incorrectly labeled as HTLV-3 discovered by Gallo.

November–December: Teams at the Pasteur Institute and the NCI map the genetic codes of both LAV and HTLV-3. The genetic codes are identical.

1985 March: The U.S. Food and Drug Administration (FDA) approves the U.S. HTLV-3 blood test.

May: Robert Gallo and the HHS are awarded a U.S. patent for their AIDS blood test.

August: Raymond Dedonder and lawyers for the Pasteur Institute formally protest the AIDS blood test patent awarded to Gallo and the HHS.

December: The Pasteur Institute sues the HHS, alleging that French, not U.S., researchers discovered the AIDS virus and that Gallo used French LAV to create his blood test.

1986 February: The FDA licenses the Pasteur Institute's AIDS blood test for sale in the United States.

May: An international committee of scientists decides that the AIDS virus will be called human immunodeficiency virus, or HIV. It will no longer be called LAV or HTLV-3.

1987 U.S. and French researchers agree to share credit for and profits from the discovery of HIV, based on a compromise proposed by world-renowned U.S. virologist Jonas Salk. Geneticist Gerald Myers discovers that the U.S. HTLV-3 and French LAV samples used to make HIV tests had come from the same patient, therefore disproving Robert Gallo's claim that he had discovered the AIDS virus and created the HIV test independently.

1990 The Office of Scientific Integrity investigates Robert Gallo's HTLV-3 research.

1992 The Office of Research Integrity concludes that Robert Gallo committed scientific misconduct by falsely reporting isolation of the AIDS virus in *Science.* The ruling is later overturned.

1994 A U.S. House of Representatives committee determines that Robert Gallo and other government officials lied about the role of U.S. scientists in the discovery of the AIDS virus and development of the AIDS test.

2002 Robert Gallo and Luc Montagnier found the Program for International Viral Collaboration to direct and fund research on an AIDS vaccine.

2008 Luc Montagnier and Françoise Barré-Sinoussi win the Nobel Prize in Medicine for their work in isolating HIV.

2011 Researchers discover that HIV-infected people can reduce transmission to noninfected people by taking antiretroviral drugs and that noninfected people can also reduce their risk of infection by taking antiretrovirals.

GLOSSARY

acquired immunodeficiency syndrome (AIDS): a disease of the human immune system characterized by a dramatic reduction of T cells, making the patient vulnerable to a variety of life-threatening illnesses

antibody: a protein created by the immune system to fight invasion by viruses and other disease-causing agents

cell: the smallest unit of living matter capable of functioning independently. Every cell from an organism contains a complete copy of an organism's deoxyribonucleic acid (DNA), or genetic coding.

cell culture: tissue or blood samples that have been removed from a person or animal and kept alive in a laboratory

deoxyribonucleic acid (DNA): a molecule in the shape of a double helix found in every living cell. DNA directs the formation, growth, and reproduction of cells and organisms.

enzyme—linked immunosorbent assay (ELISA): a blood test to determine the presence of a certain disease. The test involves exposing a patient's blood sample to a pathogen (disease-causing agent). If antibodies to the disease are present, the blood will change color. The presence of antibodies indicates that the person has been infected with the disease.

epidemic: an outbreak of disease in a short period of time within a specific community or group of people

false positive: a test result showing that a person has a disease when in fact he or she does not have it

genetic code: the sequence of genes in the DNA of an organism

growth factor: a substance that promotes growth, especially the growth of cells

HIV positive: the condition of being infected with HIV

human immunodeficiency virus (HIV): the retrovirus that causes AIDS

human T—cell leukemia virus (HTLV—3): Robert Gallo's name for HIV

immortalized cell lines: cell cultures that grow and multiply indefinitely, supplying scientists with large quantities of cells for study

immune system: the bodily system for fighting off disease

lentivirus: a slow-acting retrovirus that takes years to cause a disease and that is mainly found in animals. AIDS is the only known human lentivirus.

leukemia: a cancer of the blood in which certain blood cells begin to multiply out of control

lymphadenopathy—associated virus (LAV): Luc Montagnier's name for HIV

microbe: a microscopic organism such as a virus or bacterium

patent: a legal document giving someone the right to make, use, and sell an invention

retrovirus: a virus that can insert its genetic material into host cells, eventually taking over the host cells' reproductive functions. Some retroviruses cause cancer.

reverse transcriptase: an enzyme that enables a virus to create DNA from RNA

ribonucleic acid (RNA): a molecule that carries out genetic instructions stored in DNA

royalty: a share of the profits from an invention or creative work

T cells: white blood cells that activate other blood cells to create antibodies to fight disease

vaccine: a biological preparation that stimulates the immune system to recognize and destroy a particular disease. Vaccines usually contain a weakened or killed form of the disease against which they are designed to protect.

virus: a microscopic organism that reproduces itself only within the host cells of another living thing. Many viruses cause disease.

SOURCE NOTES

4   John Crewdson, *Science Fictions*
     (Boston: Little, Brown and Company,
     2002), 137.

5   Ibid.

11   Jonathan Engel, *The Epidemic: A Global
     History of AIDS* (New York: Smithsonian
     Books, 2006), 7.

13   Randy Shilts, *And the Band Played On:
     Politics, People and the AIDS Epidemic*
     (New York: St. Martin's Press, 1987),
     134.

13   Engel, *The Epidemic*, 7.

13   Ibid.

13   Shilts, *And the Band Played On*, 134.

15   Alan Whiteside, *HIV/AIDS: A Very Short
     History* (Oxford: Oxford University Press,
     2008), 23.

18   Robert Gallo, *Virus Hunting: AIDS,
     Cancer, and the Human Retrovirus* (New
     York: Basic Books, 1991), 47–48.

18   Crewdson, *Science Fictions*, 31.

19   Gallo, *Virus Hunting*, 19.

21   Ibid.

23   Mirko D. Grmek, *History of AIDS*
     (Princeton, NJ: Princeton University
     Press, 1990), 28.

24   Shilts, *And the Band Played On,* 263.

26   Crewdson, *Science Fictions,* 49.

26   Luc Montagnier, *Virus* (New York: W. W.
     Norton & Company, 2000), 50.

26–27 Ibid., 53.

27   Crewdson, *Science Fictions,* 49.

31   Montagnier, *Virus*, 55–56.

32   Ibid., 59.

33   Shilts, *And the Band Played On,* 372.

34   Ibid., 85.

36   Ibid., 101.

37   Ibid., 118.

39   Lawrence K. Altman, "Federal Official
     Says He Believes Cause of AIDS Has Been
     Found," *New York Times,* April 22, 1984,
     http://www.nytimes.com/1984/04/22/
     us/federal-official-says-he-believes-
     cause-of-aids-has-been-found.
     html?sec=health (March 6, 2010).

39   Shilts, *And the Band Played On,* 450–
     451.

39   Ibid.

40   Montagnier, *Virus,* 69.

40   Shilts, *And the Band Played On*, 451.

41   Montagnier, *Virus*, 73.

41   Ibid., 74.

43   Robert C. Gallo, "A Reflection on
     HIV/AIDS Research after 25 Years,"
     Retrovirology, October 20, 2006, http://
     www.retrovirology.com/content/3/1/72
     (November 17, 2011).

43   Crewdson, *Science Fictions,* 201.

43   Ibid.

47   Ibid., 227.

49–50 Ibid, 290.

50   Associated Press, "U.S. Scientist
     Confirms Mixup in AIDS Virus Study,"
     New York Times, May 31, 1991, http://
     www.nytimes.com/1991/05/31/
     news/c-us-scientist-confirms-
     mixup-in-aids-virus-study-728991
     .html?pagewanted=1 (March 12, 2010).

51   Walter Stewart, "Institutional Response
     to the HIV Blood Test Patent Dispute
     and Related Matters," *Heal,* 2009,
     http://www.healtoronto.com/starep10
     .html (November 17, 2011).

52   Ibid.

52   Associated Press, "U.S. Scientist
     Confirms Mixup in AIDS Virus Study."

53   Stewart, "Institutional Response to the
     HIV Blood Test."

53   Philip J. Hilts, "Federal Inquiry Finds
     Misconduct by a Discoverer of the AIDS

Virus," *New York Times,* December 31, 1992, http://www.nytimes.com/1992/12/31/us/federal-inquiry-finds-misconduct-by-a-discoverer-of-the-aids-virus.html?pagewanted=1 (March 12, 2010).

55 International AIDS Vaccine Initiative, "Thirty Years of AIDS Vaccine Research," *IAVIReport,* May–June 2011, http://www.iavi.org/Lists/IAVIPublications/attachments/f0c528bd-e6c0-4d28-9b68-f51100e2a34/IAVI_IAVI_REPORT_MAY-JUNE_2011_ENG.pdf (November 17, 2011).

SELECTED BIBLIOGRAPHY

Altman, Lawrence K. "Federal Official Says He Believes Cause of AIDS Has Been Found." *New York Times,* April 22, 1984. http://www.nytimes.com/1984/04/22/us/federal-official-says-he-believes-cause-of-aids-has-been-found.html?sec=health (March 6, 2010).

Associated Press. "U.S. Scientist Confirms Mixup in AIDS Virus Study." *New York Times,* May 31, 1991. http://www.nytimes.com/1991/05/31/news/c-us-scientist-confirms-mixup-in-aids-virus-study-728991.html?pagewanted=1 (March 12, 2010).

Black, David. *The Plague Years.* New York: Simon & Schuster, 1986.

Cochrane, Michelle. *When AIDS Began.* New York: Routledge, 2004.

Crewdson, John. "In Gallo Case, Truth Termed a Casualty." *Virus Myth.* January 1, 1995. http://www.virusmyth.com/aids/hiv/jcgallocase.htm (February 5, 2010).

———. *Science Fictions.* Boston: Little, Brown and Company, 2002.

Duesberg, Peter. *Inventing the AIDS Virus.* Washington, DC: Regnery, 2006.

Gallo, Robert C. *Virus Hunting: AIDS, Cancer, and the Human Retrovirus.* New York: Basic Books, 1991.

Grmek, Mirko D. *History of AIDS.* Princeton, NJ: Princeton University Press, 1990.

Hilts, Philip J. "Federal Inquiry Finds Misconduct by a Discoverer of the AIDS Virus." *New York Times,* December 31, 1992. http://www.nytimes.com/1992/12/31/us/federal-inquiry-finds-misconduct-by-a-discoverer-of-the-aids-virus.html?pagewanted=1 (March 12, 2010).

Holmberg, Scott D. *Scientific Errors and Controversies in the U.S. HIV/AIDS Epidemic.* Westport, CT: Praeger, 2008.

Kalichman, Seth C. *Denying AIDS.* New York: Spring, 2009.

Montagnier, Luc. "Autobiography." Nobel Foundation. 2008. http://nobelprize.org/nobel_prizes/medicine/laureates/2008/montagnier-autobio.html (November 17, 2011).

———. *Virus.* New York: W. W. Norton & Company, 2000.

Shilts, Randy. *And the Band Played On: Politics, People, and the AIDS Epidemic.* New York: St. Martin's Press, 1987.

Stewart, Walter. "Institutional Response to the HIV Blood Test Patent Dispute and Related Matters." *Heal.* 2009. http://www.healtoronto.com/starep10.html (November 17, 2011).

Whiteside, Alan. *HIV/AIDS: A Very Short History.* Oxford: Oxford University Press, 2008.

FOR MORE INFORMATION

BOOKS

Andrews Henningfeld, Diane, ed. *Do Infectious Diseases Pose a Threat?* Farmington Hills, MI: Lucent Books, 2009.

Cotts, Natt. *AIDS and Science.* Vestal, NY: AlphaHouse Publishing, 2008.

Currie-Mcghee, L. K. *AIDS.* Farmington Hills, MI: Lucent Books, 2008.

Goldsmith, Connie. *Invisible Invaders.* Minneapolis: Twenty-First Century Books, 2006.

Johanson, Paula. *HIV and AIDS.* New York: Rosen Publishing Group, 2007.

Jones, Phillip. *The Genetic Code.* New York: Chelsea House, 2010.

Macfarlane, Katherine. *AIDS.* Farmington Hills, MI: Greenhaven Press, 2007.

Silverstein, Alvin, Virginia Silverstein, and Laura Silverstein Nunn. *DNA.* Minneapolis: Twenty-First Century Books, 2009.

Simone, Jacquelyn. *AIDS and Politics.* New York: AlphaHouse Publishing, 2008.

Sonenklar, Carol. *AIDS.* Minneapolis: Twenty-First Century Books, 2011.

Yancy, Diane. *STDs.* Minneapolis: Twenty-First Century Books, 2011.

WEBSITES

The Age of AIDS
http://www.pbs.org/wgbh/pages/frontline/aids
This website from the Frontline series contains an explanation of AIDS, a timeline, interviews with scientists and politicians, and a map that traces the outbreak across the globe.

AIDS and HIV Information
http://www.avert.org
This comprehensive website, run by the international AIDS charity Avert, contains detailed information about HIV/AIDS around the world. The site features detailed statistics, information on protecting yourself from HIV, scientific and historical information, and a country-by-country breakdown of the epidemic.

HIV/AIDS among Youth
http://www.cdc.gov/hiv/resources/factsheets/youth.htm
This site, run by the Centers for Disease Control and Prevention, is a comprehensive source of information about HIV/AIDS for young people. The site lists HIV/AIDS statistics, risk factors, and prevention information.

Red Gold: The Epic Story of Blood
http://www.pbs.org/wnet/redgold
Based on a popular PBS television show, this site covers the science of human blood, historical discoveries in research, and new challenges concerning AIDS. The section on innovators and pioneers contains information about Robert Gallo, Luc Montagnier, and others who are central to the HIV/AIDS story.

LERNER

SOURCE

Expand learning beyond the printed book. Download free, complementary educational resources for this book from our website, www.lernerresource.com.

INDEX

PHOTO ACKNOWLEDGMENTS

ABOUT THE AUTHOR

Over the past twenty years, Stuart A. Kallen has written more than 250 nonfiction books for children and young adults. His books have covered many aspects of human history, culture, and science, from the building of the pyramids to the music of the twenty-first century. Some of his recent titles include *The Aftermath of the Sandinista Revolution; Postmodern Art; We Are Not Beasts of Burden: Cesar Chavez and the Delano Grape Strike, California, 1965–1970; Open the Jail Doors—We Want to Enter: The Defiance Campaign Against Apartheid Laws, South Africa, 1952; Vampire History and Lore;* and *Che Guevara: You Win or You Die.* Kallen, who lives in San Diego, California, is also a singer-songwriter and guitarist.